Inhalt

Herstellung und Publisher:

© 2019
Herstellung und Publisher: BoD – Books on Demand, Norderstedt.
ISBN: 9783749464623

Copyright:
© 2019 Taylor E. Baxter,
Erstveröffentlichung 22.4.2019

[6]

foreword

Many players do without training and are extremely disappointed because they are constantly on the way to respawn or scarcely score any goals.

> ➢ Do you want to win?

> ➢ Do you dream of great victories and excellent hit rates?

> ➢ Do you want a fantastic performance?

> ➢ Do you see yourself chasing opponents across the field after a long matchday?

If you answer these questions with yes, training is useful and sensible for you.

Volume 3 is your basis for meaningful and successful Airsoft training. You get tips and tricks to get physically fitter, how to use your markers in the best possible way and how to achieve higher hit rates.

Every beginning is difficult, take your first steps and start your personal training! How to find it here!

__Why Training?__

You certainly know the saying "No master has fallen from the sky".

To achieve a goal, training and automated movements help. If you have a driver's license, think about driving a car.

In the beginning, it's hard and all sorts of things come crashing down on you. Many novice drivers tremble when they think of road traffic!

After some time they have good to excellent safety and don't have to worry about many things anymore because they have internalized them.

Training in Airsoft is similar.

You can read about tactics and watch movies - as long as you don't master them, it's hard to implement them.

Many people enjoy watching sports but don't do it. If for various reasons they are forced to set up their own activities, they get out of breath. The whole theory is of little help here.

Training helps you to catapult yourself physically as well as in knowledge, and thus to beat other players more easily.

Why do people train?

We have tons of technical support in all sorts of matters and yet people take the trouble and sometimes the torture of training upon themselves.

Good gear is a great thing. But even the best equipment is of little use if you run out of breath after 15 minutes and are finished.

Training helps you to improve, develop and defeat your opponent!

That's why athletes, musicians, chess players and everyone else trains. The only difference is in what they train. Why do people train?

Think of the successful teams in Airsoft. The best of them have knowledge, skills and are well coordinated.

Think of yourself:

- o Do you start sweating immediately at the slightest movement?
- o Do you think you can keep up a whole matchday?
- o Why do you think you are physically able to pack Airsoft?

Basically, there are two possibilities!

Pack less gear and equipment and make your luggage lighter! Buy a lighter marker and do without manual sniper rifles.

<u>OR</u>

Train your fitness before you start Airsoft. The body learns quickly. It doesn't take a masterstroke to be a marathon - start with regular walks.

Couch potatoes easily underestimate their actual performance. After a few meters of sprinting, the air is out, the heart is racing and the circulation begins to spin.

Do you want to spend the rest of the day in the safe zone or in the hospital?

The first day of the game will be remembered. How will you remember it later?

Tip:

Train yourself a basic condition! All the equipment you buy for a lot of money won't help you much if your fitness is in trouble.

Think realistically about what your body can do. People have a natural tendency towards coziness!

Move regularly, in smaller doses, do without lifts and climb stairs. Get yourself a dog!

It's the little things that lay the foundation!

Everyone starts differently. Find your perfect start! Adapt the gear to you and your needs, plan the right training for you. Combine both! Train together with others in a team.

The combination counts, one component is not enough!

Your Training

With training, you achieve better performance.

Are there Airsoft players who don't care whether they win or lose? Most people play Airsoft to have fun, exercise and win.

A first aspect to prepare for your training is to choose your equipment and your marker. Later you will be able to use them in training!

High quality equipment

If you are unsure whether Airsoft is your sport, start with a cheap marker. Later, more expensive, better models make more sense. A powerful, reliable marker that meets your needs is more expensive than a model-out-of-the-box.

In return, you get something that suits you better! Choose wisely which model you plan for your future main marker! High-quality markers cost more to start with.

Take more money for your second marker and choose a high-quality model! Poor quality markers will slow you down, give up and cause problems due to softer metal and poorer quality

protective gear

This includes matching glasses, a good headgear, arm and leg protection and much more. Make sure your protective equipment is of high quality.

[12]

Above all, pay attention to high-quality eye protection! You have a pair of eyes that cannot be replaced.

Focus on quality! The purchase of good protective equipment is a must-have!

Select suitable markers

A good portion of Airsoft beginners chooses a marker after the optics. They see them in movies or use them in computer games. Due to a large number of manufacturers, the same "weapon model" differs in price and quality.

Don't just go for the optics! Ask experienced players if they recommend the brand to you! For example, 10 years ago a marker of the "Systema" brand was considered expensive and of high quality, today they have overtaken other brands.

Some Airsoft shops offer the opportunity to try out markers. Occasionally associations offer "rental markers".

Do you prefer heavier models (machine guns, sniper models, ...) or do you tend towards lighter markers (CQB, Thompson, Grease, ...)?

Do you like modern or older "models" better? Could you imagine playing with a BAR or a Grease or are you interested in markers with many rail tracks?

Wrongly chosen markers frustrate and prevent good performance on your part.

Your performance

The main purpose of the training is to improve your performance and therefore your performance.

Find a mentor who will teach you tricks! Anyone who loves Airsoft and/or has experience in the military or police can teach you good things!

Practice regularly

Nothing comes from nothing! Train regularly! Internal movement sequences in your muscle memory until the movement runs automatically!

If you train solo, have trained players regularly checked by experienced players or your mentor. Wrongly trained sequences are hard to get out of muscle memory.

Military Training

Fitness centers and fashion sports are booming. What sport have you been doing so far? Were you playing football, running or hiking? Do you do martial arts? Did you lift weights in the gym? Airsoft offers you a lot from classic sports and additional interesting components!

Comparison of sports!

In most sports, you need stamina, discipline and the will to achieve concrete goals. If you train "only" to get rid of annoying kilos, for example, you often lack the fun and you end up quitting again. If, for example, you train for a running event like the marathon, you will continue because it is important to you.

Without motivation, you will soon stop doing sport - it doesn't matter which sport it is.

Military style training means a change in "normal" life. Through this kind of training, you will gain self-confidence, your life will change in a positive way and last but not least you will gain strength and strength to cope with difficult everyday situations in a positive way.

Take a closer look at "Military Training". Both men and women train their bodies first in boot camps - many civilians lack physical strength, endurance or discipline.

The next step is to strengthen your personality, overcome (personal) boundaries and lead entire teams.

Take a look at the "team building measures" of various companies. In many cases, superiors force their subordinates to do childish exercises at different levels, which the employees enjoy in the best case scenario.

Bosses want functioning teams and try to weld them together with various seminars. With "military training" you achieve this in a simpler way in a team. If you're in a team, or if you're thinking of joining an existing team, give the impetus!

Military style training!

The basics of "military training" can be found above all in physical fitness programs! If you find yourself in a gym from time to time, these points will certainly look familiar to you.

Train like a military man!

- ✓ *Go running*
  Create a matching mixture of jogging, running and sprinting!
  This will increase your speed and endurance.
  Interval training is a good choice!
- ✓ *Go hiking*
  With what amount of luggage on your back are you fit enough to march for a long time? Accustom yourself to longer hikes with a heavy backpack. In the beginning, several bottles of water are enough. Increase your weight when you're ready. In the long run, a basic weight of 15 - 30 kg is suitable.
  Hiking strengthens your back, feet, ankles and various muscle groups.
- ✓ *Start pull-ups and/or slopes with bent arms*
  These exercises train your upper body and strengthen you! In Airsoft there are obstacles to overcome which you can overcome more easily with more power.
- ✓ *Do abdominal muscle exercises*
  One of the most essential main components of IST and PFT is a strengthened body center. Strengthening

abdominal muscle exercises help prevent back injuries and help you purchase a "six pack".

✓ *Rounding off and completing basic training*
  Sit-Ups, Chrunches, Planks and lifting of the legs, Squats, Lunges and Crucifixions

Get a proper diet!

If you train more often, you usually change your diet. Adapt your eating habits to the new situation.

- ✓ Focus more on healthy carbohydrates, proteins and fats.
- ✓ Reduce sugar, extremely fatty foods and preservatives as much as possible.
- ✓ Drink enough, you will need the liquid! Prefer electrolyte drinks, mix tap water with apple juice or get Recruit Gatorade.

Find your „Drillseargent"!

Do you manage to do your training alone or do you need someone to motivate you? You don't need to be a soldier. Look around for a fitness trainer to accompany you. Find a motivated training partner who will flush you out if you don't feel like it. If you have a girlfriend, start regular jogging with her!

The early bird catches the worm!

As a rule, successful people start their day before the others. They get up earlier, at a time when they are fresh and rested. In our "sleep-in society" long sleep is popular. Those who wait too long shouldn't be surprised when they wobble on the couch in the evening and are too exhausted for everything.

Literatur and Shows

Good training books are like sand by the sea. You can find different training channels on Youtube and in the "normal" TV program.

Suitable literature and harmonious programs are ideal for putting together your own personal training program.

The books/shows/channels presented here are basic tips for your training program. Expand them and expand them as you like! Within a short time, you will recognize which exercises suit you best!

This includes physical training units as well as "marker drill" and tactical units!

Set your own priorities! With the books/shows/channel suggested here, you will find a basic coverage of the entire need!

Buchtipps:

The Complete Guide to Navy Seal Fitness, Third Edition: Updated for Today's Warrior Elite by Stewart Smith USN (SEAL) (2008-01-15) (mit DVD!)

- o **Paperback**: 208 Pages
- o **Publisher:** Hatherleigh Press; Circulation: Updated (15. January 2008)
- o **Language:** English
- o **ISBN-10:** 1578262666

MARSOC Training Guide: The Official US Marine Corps Special Operations Physical Fitness Handbook: Get Marine Fit in 10 Weeks

- o **Paperback:** 76 Pages
- o **Publisher:** CreateSpace Independent Publishing Platform; Circulation: 1 (3. November 2017)
- o **Language:** English
- o **ISBN-10:** 1979225001

The United States Marine Corps Workout (Five Star Official Fitness Guides)

- o **Paperback:** 224 Pages
- o **Publisher:** Hatherleigh Press; Circulation: Rev (20. February 2004)
- o **Language:** English
- o **ISBN-10:** 1578261589

The Ultimate Marine Recruit Training Guidebook: A Drill Instructor's Strategies and Tactics for Success

- o **Paperback:** 192 Pages
- o **Publisher:** Savas Beatie (19. Juni 2012)
- o **Language:** English
- o **ISBN-10:** 1932714731

The book trade offers training books on a wide variety of topics. Although most of them offer good to excellent tips, military training reading is primarily suitable for rapid (Airsoft) success. You train the muscle groups you need for successful Airsoft!

Military training books focus on the basics! That's why they make sense for your beginning!

Choose wisely which training books you think to make sense for you!

Tip:

Pay attention to these three components::

- o Quick, target-oriented success
- o easy, efficient exercises
- o little to zero equipment

TV-Tips:

Eine Woche in der Trainingshölle
(Special Forces – Ultimate Hell Week)

How do Special Forces train? For all those who don't like to deal with books, a look at the British show "Special Forces Bootcamp" is suitable.

British civilians gained their first personal experience of different training methods of different special units.

To belong to the best you don't need a pure material battle. Players do not need to be tactical geniuses. However, a certain basis of physical fitness makes sense.

It is not even necessary to find special units great. The training methods are interesting! Much of it can be used and implemented for your own "build-up training".

Season 1

- o Episode 1 (Navy Seals - USA)
- o Episode 2 (Yamam - Israel)
- o Episode 3 (Navsog - Philippines)
- o Episode 4 (SAS - Australia)
- o Episode 5 (Spetznaz - Russia)
- o Episode 6 (SAS – Great Britain)

Season 2

- o Episode 7 (Recces – South Africa)
- o Episode 8 (GROMS – Polend)
- o Episode 9 (Green Berets – USA)
- o Episode 10 (ROK UDT – South Korea)
- o Episode 11 (GIGN – France)
- o Episode 12 (SASR – Australia)

Wichtig zu beachten:

There are amazing parallels in "recruit training" between the various special units.

This includes exercises as well as the handling of recruits.

Presented training units belong to the "basic training" of the new recruits in the respective units!

Naturally, some, a few days do not replace the actual, complete training, especially if it lasts several months. However, the programme offers a short, interesting insight!

If you want inspiration and ideas for your own training, this show is perfect! If you don't have much time to put together a training plan, all you need is this show for an absolute base!

Bomber Boys – The Fighting Lancaster

This Canadian production, shot in 2005, illuminates the "Bomber Boys - The Fighting Lancaster" in more detail.

The grandchildren of the former unit live through all the training sessions in this show like their grandfathers did in the 40s. They wear the same clothes, receive the same nutrition and train according to the same guidelines as their grandfathers. They learn the discipline and values of a past era.

In between, the veterans talk about the night sky over occupied Europe and the battles in which they flew. In this way, they create the link to the popular series "Band of Brothers".

After the show, the generations meet again. Modern people, who have understood many of the problems and difficulties of the grandfather generation, meet the veterans, whose pride in their achievements in the liberation of Europe is understandable!

Everyone who trains leaves his "comfort zone" first. It is often an overcoming not to go to the comfortable couch after training and to leave the television switched off.

Participants in a broadcast format such as "Bomber Boys" then step into a new life for them. Training and the feeling of another epoch change for the better and strengthen the character.

SOE-Training – Churchills Geheimagenten – Die Neuen

In the Second World War, a new organization, the "Special Operations Executive" (SOE), came into service. Spies in Churchill's service had a serious influence on the course of World War II. They led acts of sabotage, eliminated high-ranking National Socialists at the risk of their lives and much more.

Hundreds of average civilians benefited from exclusive SOE training designed specifically for the SOE. It thus laid the foundation for the training methods of later military units.

In addition to British civilians, hundreds of Americans received this training, took it over and built the military training known today from it in the episodic decades!

The special thing about this unit:

- ✓ *equality*
  Men and women trained in exactly the same standards.
- ✓ *Innovative*
  methods used were based on a wide variety of successful aspects and formed a harmonious, new whole
- ✓ *effectiveness*
  These methods brought the students to their limits within a very short time and showed the true core in their innermost being.

„Churchills Geheimagenten – Die Neuen" you'll find on Netflix. This show is recommended for anyone who is thinking about historical training and plans to create their own training plan based on it.

Is it feasible for modern participants to become a successful SOE agent by the standards of that time? 14 participants started the program, learned how to handle explosives, physical fitness training, survival training, radio training and much more.

Versatile preparation helped SOE agents to achieve eruptions in the occupied countries and created the basis for a more peaceful future!

For your training program, the aspects of physical training such as "self-crossing methods" are the most important.

Training sequences in films

Independent of various documentaries and shows, there are also films with military programs. It doesn't matter whether the film offers a good or a bad plot. Focus on the "training sequences"!

Watch all the movies with different eyes. As a rule, like most movies, you're more likely to notice the storyline or action scenes. There's nothing wrong with that. If you are specifically looking for training sequences, you need a different perspective.

These films are examples of other sources of inspiration.

- o ***G.I. Jane (die Akte Jane) / Major Movie Star***
  (Female) main characters successfully undergo a
  military training program.
- o ***Full Metal Jacket***
  This strip stands for "typical" drill instructor films.
- o ***Die 36 Kammern der Shaolin***
  Asian films sometimes show hard training methods.
  Take them for inspiration, but not too seriously! Films
  by "Chackie Chan" or "Bruce Lee" also fall into this
  category!
- o ***Dr. Strange / X-Men – First Class***
  A lot of people like to watch superhero movies.
  Thousands of viewers love them idolatrously. In some
  of them, you'll find inspiration for your own training.

During training, no matter which you choose, it is important to leave your comfort zone and become active!

Put your energy and courage together and get going!

Train your body and learn to persevere. What generations before us have done, you pack just as well. It's not a question of age or your current fitness status, but a question of will and discipline.

You are your own boss, your own drill sergeant, your own fitness trainer. If you decide to start your training, it's time to start! Not tomorrow, not in a week, but today!

Tomorrow everything may have changed. TODAY is the right moment, TODAY is the right day. Get up and get moving.

[28]

Channels:

You know Full Metal Jacket for sure. R. Lee Ermey coined the idea of a typical "Drill instructor" with his presentation of the Drill-Instructor Gunnery Sergeant Hartman!

Did you know that he had his own Youtube channel?

Title of the Channel:
Lock n' Load with R. Lee Ermey

Independently of this, he moderated the show "Mail Call" since 2002. Erme answered questions from viewers about weapons, equipment, customs and terminology from all branches of the US military.

He led viewers to military training areas, filmed demonstrations and consulted with other experts.

His set resembled a military outpost with tent, jeep and various equipment. Sometimes there was a bulldog at his side, a symbol of the Marines. He acted like a typical drill instructor with the viewer and entertained the audience in a grandiose way. His behavior sometimes resembled the character of his role as Gunnery Sergeant Hartman.

If you're looking for a "role model" in the form of a drill instructor, Lee Ermey is an excellent choice. High-level knowledge about weapons and the lasting impression of his role as Gunnery Sergeant Hartman made him an impressive capacity for anyone who deals with "military training"!

Ermey belonged to the USMC from 1961 to 1971 and had real war experience through his work in the Vietnam War. After his retirement, he studied criminology and theatre studies at the "University of Manila".

Francis Ford Coppola engaged him as a military advisor. From this time he was part of the American film world!

In 2002 he was promoted to the rank of "Gunnery Seargent". So far, he is the first and only Marine to be promoted out of service - and rightly so!

Physical Training

Is there already a training plan in your mind? Do you already know which exercises you will integrate?

Preparation is everything!

Often the first thought is to run into a sports shop and buy everything you need for training! To a certain extent, this is correct. But you don't have to spend a fortune on your training!

Type of training and associated training location

In the USA, various private organizations now offer Bootcamp-oriented training courses.

If you orientate yourself on classic boot camp training, you have the option to split the training sessions. Use forests, cities and your own body!

Get background literature and training manuals from the American military (Special Forces, Navy Seals, Army, MASOC, ...). You'll find effective training sessions that push you forward quickly!

Take a look at series like "Special Forces Bootcamp", adopt the training methods that seem to make sense for you. The participants don't need chic, hip sports clothes, but wear useful clothes.

Practical clothing, suitable footwear and yourself are enough to start with the fitness aspect. Combine push-ups, sit-ups and knee bend with running. Especially forest soil is suitable. It is softer than asphalt, you protect your ankles and kneecaps and have the advantage of uneven ground.

For strength training, you can use a fitness center, dumbbells from a sports shop or your own marker.

In "military training" you need above all the will to tackle the training and to hold out. You don't need to leave a fortune in a sports shop!

Running Cadences

Put together the right rhythmic support. A wide variety of running cadences is suitable for this. Listen to the military as they run!

As a rule, one person in the group will give a sentence and the others will shout it out. The lyrics sound banal but help to keep the rhythm because of their beat.

simple basic training for beginners

How often have you started and given up fitness training?

Man is by nature a creature of habit and comfort. The inner pig makes things even more difficult!

Slower changes are easier than bigger ones. The desire for a "six-pack" or a certain basic fitness is there.

How often do such plans stand on New Year's Eve wishes and are discarded within a short time again? Right after New Year's Eve, fitness centers are massively overcrowded - for a few weeks!

Pay attention to the fun factor in training! It doesn't matter WHAT you train, the important thing is THAT you train!

Airsoft appeals to most muscle groups. A certain basic fitness helps you so that you don't lose the fun of Airsoft immediately!

Start small!

Very few of us have the opportunity to train in a boot camp. The advantage would be the absolute concentration on the training with simultaneous shielding from distractions outside.

Most trainers know the problem of integrating training units into their everyday lives! We have jobs and families that demand. If you assemble a mega-project, the whole plan will collapse like a house of cards within a short time.

If you don't have any training experience, start with small doses. The intensity can be increased at any time!

Daily start:

- ✓ 10 push-ups
- ✓ 10 Sit-up
- ✓ 10 knee bends
- ✓ 1x a week a longer distance after choice go

If the workload is too slow for you, switch to the next step. Increase the number of exercises from 10 to 15 or integrate additional exercises!

missing Motivation

Each of us has days where it is no fun to train or where we are too tired and ticks differently. Trainers need different methods to get closer to their "training goal". Pick the methods that suit you. If you don't know them, try them out until you have the solution!

Set yourself concrete goals

Is there something you want to achieve and/or have? Would you stop halfway or if it was within reach? This tip is primarily for beginners.

Set goals and timings. Don't overstrain yourself in the beginning, but be realistic! No master has fallen from the sky yet.

Imagine you are a character in a computer game who collects experience. It will fail as a beginner before the boss rather than an experienced warrior or magician. Physical training is the same! Set yourself realistic goals! If you overtax yourself within a short time, you lose your motivation and thus the fun of the thing.

Let your inner child train!

Children like to move by nature as long as they are not physically restricted. You can make even stupid, boring training more "childlike". For example, when you're running, imagine overcoming obstacles from computer games. Jump over stones or run slalom around trees - "Gamify" your training!

try out new methods and locations

Constantly training the same boring. Run different routes and at different times of the day. Try different equipment in a fitness center. Check out training manuals. Test out what appeals to you. You'll get a lot of muscle soreness this way, but at the same time, you'll find training methods that suit you. There are different exercises for strengthening almost every muscle group!

Training is far more than setting the body in motion.

Why do military units train and drill prospective soldiers?

Physical training offers more than just physical improvement. They also train the mind!

As soon as you realize that you can increase your training level, you experience Episode. You learn patience and discipline through more boring training sessions.

Seek support

Many have a problem training alone. They need someone who motivates them and shoos them up on days when they don't feel like it or when they are exhausted from work. If you are this type, look for a training partner.

Feedback

Give yourself feedback! Design it constructively. Analyze your own performance and think about possible improvements. Don't be afraid to ask others for help if you are unsure or want a countercheck. Be honest with yourself!

medical checkup

If you are at the beginning, a medical check in the form of a health examination is recommended. Know your health status so that you don't experience any nasty surprises.

Plan pauses on

The body needs rest periods after a strenuous workout. During this time the body recovers and uses the time to regenerate and strengthen weakened muscles.

If you plan daily training, make sure that you address different muscle groups! For example Monday - upper body training, Tuesday - running, Wednesday - leg muscles, ...

Be your own trainingspartner

Your toughest opponent is yourself, for example in shadow boxing or when you keep a training book and compare when you did what.

Of course, there are other methods of how you can build up your (physical) training. Listen to your gut feeling, pay attention to your body and don't overstrain it. Be careful with the under straining, which is boring fast and gives you no further stimulation.

Tips for your training!

Military methods are constant and effective. No frills are needed, your own body is usually sufficient. Besides the training, there are some aspects to consider!

Training generally

- ✓ *hydration*
  Drink enough water! Dehydration happens fast!
- ✓ *small portions of food*
  Eat smaller portions at regular intervals. Too much at once will hurt you!
- ✓ *Salt and sugar packs (from MRE packs)*
  Mix both in water. This will give you the "Recruit Gatorade". It supplements sweaty minerals better than many "sports drinks".
- ✓ *The challenge is for the mind, not the body.*
  Force yourself to stay concentrated and focused, don't let the herd guide you!
- ✓ *Take personal responsibility*
  Don't be afraid of your own decisions, you learn and profit from mistakes and failure!
- ✓ *Watch your feet!*
  You are on your way on them. Give them the chance to recover. Take off boots and socks, massage them briefly. You'll do better on long stretches if you give your feet good things to do.

Training with trainingpartners

✓ *Perform learning*
   Prove that you can reliably execute other people's orders. This is all the truer if you don't know the reason. In the military (and in Airsoft games) you don't always know the reason for an action!

✓ *Equipment check*
   If you train with Gear, check each other out. Make your comrade aware if you see anything loose or broken. He may not have discovered it yet! If you conceal it, you are (partly) responsible for its (mis)success.

IST, PFT and CFT

Do you know your personal fitness status yet?

Here IST, PFT, and CFT offer themselves to experience your own fitness status.

An essential characteristic of Special Forces units and the military, in general, are demands on physical fitness and endurance!

IST – Initial Strength Test

- *Pull-ups/Hangs with bent arms*
  Men - 2 full pull-ups
  Women - 12 Seconds hold with bent arms
- *Crunches*
  Men like women need to create 44 crunches (elbows or forearms to the knees) in 2 minutes
- *Laufen auf Zeit*
  Men - 1,5 Miles (2,4km) in 13:30 Minutes
- Women - 1.5 Miles (2.4km) in 15 minutes

PFT - Physical Fitness Test

If you are over 26 years old, the criteria are correspondingly lower!

- *Pull-ups/Hangs with bent arms*
  Men - 3 full pull-ups
  Women - 15 Seconds hold with bent arms

➢ *Crunches*
  Men like women need to create 50 crunches (elbows or forearms to the knees) in 2 minutes.
➢ *Run for time*
  Men - 3 Miles (about 4.8km) in 28 minutes
➢ Women - 3 Miles (ca. 4,8km) in 31 Minutes

CFT – Combat Fitness Test

The maximum score of 100 points with a maximum of 300 points. The minimum number is calculated on the basis of age and gender.

➢ *Battle Movements*
  The obstacle course of 880 yards (approx. 805m)
  Maximum score Men - 2:45 Minutes
  Maximum score Women - 3:23 Minutes
➢ *Lifting ammunition*
  Men - 91 repetitions
  Women - 61 repetitions
➢ *maneuvers under fire*
  This includes exercises such as running, sneaking, carrying or throwing grenades.
  Maximum score Men - 2:14 Minutes
  Maximum score Women - 3:01 Minutes

Where you at? Can you do all three?

How does a Bootcamp work?

In a boot camp, civilians turn into fighters, soldiers and comrades. You don't have to adjust it 1 to 1! Learn how military training works to perfect your own.

Week 1 - Reception

- ✓ paperwork management
- ✓ Cutting the hair
- ✓ Preparations for wage receipt
- ✓ Medical and dental demonstrations
- ✓ Placement on the basis of various initial tests

Week 2 - Barracks / Barracks

- ✓ The practice of a concrete drill
- ✓ Life after fixed times -> from brushing your teeth to going to sleep

Week 3 - Bayonet Drill

- ✓ bayonet fight

Week 4 - Fight

- ✓ basic USMC martial arts
- ✓ Familiarization with the core values of USMC
- ✓ Completion of the 3-Miles-Marches with a final confidence run
- ✓ daily participation of recruits in physical training
- ✓ academic classes

Week 5 - Martial Arts - MCMAP (Marine Corps Martial Arts Program)

- ✓ Week 5 - Martial Arts - MCMAP (Marine Corps Martial Arts Program)
- ✓ self-defense training
- ✓ Martial Arts History
- ✓ Marine Corps values (mental and physical resilience)
- ✓ Water Survival Training
- ✓ 5-Miles Hike
- ✓ First aid skills

Week 6 - rapid abseiling

- ✓ Learning techniques for safe rapid abseiling

Week 7 – Outdoor

- ✓ Weapon training with an M16
- ✓ Dry training, followed by sharp ammunition
- ✓ Shot positions: standing, kneeling, sitting and lying

Week 8 - Sharp weapons

- ✓ single shot
- ✓ 10 shots in the episode
- ✓ If the qualifications are fulfilled, the prospective navy receives the title/designation "Rifle Marksman badge", "Rifle Sharpshooter badge" or the coveted "Rifle Expert badge".

Week 9 - Trust course

- ✓ Implementation of the learned within 45 minutes in combination with an obstacle course consisting of 11 different obstacles, one heavier than the other.

Week 10 - Movement

- ✓ Simulated combat operations
- ✓ Learning further basics
- ✓ 3 day Basic Warrior Training

Week 11 - The Crucible - Hell Week

- ✓ Application of everything learned so far under massively tightened conditions
  Test duration: 54 hours

Week 12 – Graduation

- ✓ Whoever makes it this far can call himself a Marine!

A boot camp works because it trains recruits in a wide variety of areas. They are away from their daily routine and concentrate only on the training.

In many cases, recruits end this way if they think they can't make it. No matter where they left off, they benefit from what they have learned and taken it with them into their lives after the boot camp!

What can you learn from a boot camp?

Basically, you can learn something in every situation and take it with you into your future.

The focal points of a boot camp are clearly marked and given. You see what they bring and how they help you to improve your Airsoft skills.

Take a look at the series episode of the weeks!

Nobody expects you to get the championship title immediately. You'll get it if you put what you've learned into perfect practice.

A boot camp primarily shows which steps you should start with.

Tip:
Learn theory!
Train your body!
Use a game for "hell week"! Prove yourself there! Are you able to put everything you have learned into practice?

Teamtraining

Most people find it difficult to train solo or to begin with.

Training in a team is fun, you interact with each other and you apply tactics and training methods in the team that a "single" trainer is denied.

If you are thinking about becoming part of a team, ask if that team trains together.

Team training has the advantage that the individual participants get to know each other better. This has a positive effect on later player episodes.

Well coordinated teams win on average more often than those who rarely or never train together.

It is difficult to reconcile working people (especially if this family has one). Don't let it stop you. Most have commitments that are difficult for them to avoid.

Do your best!

Team-Training

After setting up a team, it is time to train together. Team training helps to improve one's own skills and at the same time strengthens team cohesion. Every athlete recognizes the need for training to develop and improve their performance. It is up to you what and how you build the training.

There are many different ways to train a team. What works for one team doesn't necessarily work for another. If teams train together, they tune in to each other in the course of the training.

Trainingmanagement

Effective training usually requires someone to lead this training. The person should have experience. Whether military, policeman, experienced airsoft player or fitness trainer plays no role! It is important that you have a certain basic structure! Building on this, modules and elements can be built into the training.

The task of a training leader is difficult! He passes on his knowledge in the appropriate quantity. Initially, the team consists of different training levels. His task is to adjust the levels of the trainers to each other without neglecting anyone.

Since Airsoft is based on the military theme, this training leader can certainly orient himself on a typical drill instructor.

[48]

Their task is to prepare the recruits physically, mentally and spiritually for their later tasks.

Physical Training

Use the IST, PFT or CFT during training. The training leader finds out where the individual trainers are at the moment.

Classical fitness training such as running, sit-up or push-ups helps to achieve a uniform level.

This simple basic training welds the players together and helps to achieve a higher level of physical fitness.

Tactical Training

Do you know where you're going to play first? Each field has different requirements. In addition to physical training, it makes sense to train in these fields. Experience has shown that these initial combinations are a good choice.

- *gravel pit* -> running training, sprinting
- *meadows with coverings* -> running training, sprinting
- *Houses and/or halls* -> Schleichen
- *Forest* -> Sneaking, training the upper arms, camouflaging

Expand your training! Adapt it! You will find more aspects and combinations that make sense for the terrain.

Communicationtraining

Communicates with each other. If you use radio, learn to use it! Train the radio alphabet! Pay attention to the correct channel and think about which codes you will use. Without radios, you'll need hand signals or other signals that only you know.

Research and training selection

Fitness training is popular around the globe. There are non-fiction books of different methods to choose from. Check out Youtube videos or talk to fitness trainers.

For Airsoft, training documents of real units are ideal. These can be bought in bookstores and offer a wealth of information.

On TV and Youtube, you will find a wide variety of formats showing military training. These include various documentaries and "shows" such as "Special Forces Bootcamp", "Bomber Boys" or "SOE - Churchill's Secret Agents - The New".

In all three shows, you can see how often unknowns come together to form a great team. Pick out the right training units for you and train according to the methods you choose!

Attract Experienced People

Is there anyone in your environment with a military or police background? These people have useful knowledge, know about tactics and physical fitness training. Ask if they train you. In the worst case, they say no. If they decide to train you, help yourselves! Such chances are rare. If they agree, you have a decisive knowledge advantage that you can use in favor of your team in Airsoft.

Copy what works

Look at successful and experienced teams. What tactics do they use? What do they do when they play? Copy the methods that work! Watch them on the field, watch Youtube videos! Read testimonials and learn from them! Copy their successful strategies!

Build your own strategies

If tactics work for a team, it doesn't mean they work for you. Each team has different merits. Who do you have in your team? Experienced athletes have different skills than computer players or couch potatoes who constantly watch movies.

Copying others will do you a lot of good if you adopt these tactics and methods to yourselves. Simple copying without adapting is of little use!

Distinguish between theoretical and practical skills/knowledge

Do you have the knowledge to read maps, radio or analyze tactics? Get a folder or notebook and write down what you learn. Use it to create your own "roadmap" to help newcomers to the game.

Formulate information from videos, books, or other sources in your words, but understandable enough to communicate with others.

Go through the topics with your team, let them ask questions. If you can't answer at the moment, you know the weak points of your current knowledge!

Tip:

Keep the information short, compact and concise. Proceed methodically!

Use training aids like flyers! What has worked for you in school lessons? Use these methods. Remember, there are different types of learners!

If, for example, you learn the radio alphabet, you train it by practicing radio. Pure dry training is of no use to many. Knowledge of theory with subsequent practical exercises is a good idea in advance.

If you learn to read maps, you can do an orienteering run afterward! If you practice sparks, then study the radio alphabet until it sits.

[52]

Theory and practice work best in a combination pack!

Tip:
Tip:

Keep the information short, compact and concise. Proceed methodically!

Use training aids like flyers! What has worked for you in school lessons? Use these methods. Remember, there are different types of learners!

For example, if you learn the funk alphabet, you train it by practicing sparks. Pure dry training is of no use to many. Knowledge of theory with subsequent practical exercises is a good idea in advance.

If you learn to read maps, you can do an orienteering run afterward! If you practice sparks, then study the radio alphabet until it sits. Theory and practice work best in a combination pack!

If your physical team training is planned, there are two possibilities:

1. _regular meetings_
   The catch is, the players need time regularly. Many have family and professions that challenge them. The bigger the team, the harder it is to call these meetings all the time.
2. _meet from time to time_
   Think about individual training steps and practice them for one day. The "practice", until it sits, each player takes over for himself, if he finds the time for it. Meet

at regular intervals to check your progress. These meetings are important to check if you are training an exercise incorrectly.

One-to-one training is a waste of time because many people need training partners! If necessary, you can form mini teams and train in double packs, for example.

Train under realistic conditions. The muscle memory thanks it.

Learn how to handle your markings. Build indoor shooting boxes, learn to aim. Do regular shooting exercises. Practice fast magazine changes.

The safer you handle your marker, the easier it will be for you!

Conclusion

Trained under realistic conditions. The muscle memory thanks it.

Learn how to handle your markings. Build indoor firing boxes, learn to aim. Do regular shooting exercises. Practice fast magazine changes.

The safer you handle your marker, the easier it will be for you!

There are many ways to get the training you need. Expect realistic results in the beginning. Someone who has been sitting in front of a PC for years sweats more at first and tires more quickly. Others are endurance runners who lack strength.

Human bodies are not machines! Everyone has a starting base in which they have trained certain structures, skills, and abilities. Whether this is the operation of a computer mouse or a strong abdominal musculature, there is something to be done with everything!

The goal is to train the team on each other. In every team, you will find players who are willing to give up quickly because they think they need the mega performance of a trained special soldier right from the start. The body needs time!

As long as you have a base to build on, you've already achieved a lot.

tactics

Many players love "run-shoot" games. These are especially fun for beginners and a great warm-up option for everyone. Players with more gaming experience sometimes wonder if it was. They ask for more.

Those who decide to participate in a MilSim often think long in advance about the different tactics they intend to use. Take tactics from blockbuster movies only conditionally seriously. Such films need an action-packed storyline and sometimes use tactics that do not work in reality in this form.

Have you ever dealt with military literature? Different textbooks and different educational films guide you in basic tactics. Remember, not every military tactic works the same in Airsoft. On the one hand, it is because of missing play areas (gravel pits, forest, meadows, houses, ...) on the other hand Airsoft markers do not have the range of real weapons.

Forget Computer Games

Most of us love to sit at the computer and play. Remember, the computer is not a real opponent! On the computer, you click the mouse button, aim at the opponent's head because it scores the best points, pull the trigger and voila - the opponent is history! It doesn't work in Airsoft!

This example also works in connection with military tactics! Adapt them to your needs in the best possible way!

Don't transfer computer games 1 to 1 to Airsoft.

[56]

It's better to look at real historical events. What actions did soldiers use?

Watch documentaries.

If you're more into movies and series, Band of Brothers or NAM - Call of Duty is the place for a first, helpful look.

Learning by doing

Above all - try it out! But there is a catch!

You need players who don't follow the "Lone Wolf" pattern but act in a team. Tactics are usually a "team thing".

Beginners, who have hardly or not yet dealt with military tactics and procedures, achieve individual hits. Real "experts" use tactics and thus achieve much more!

Beginners often lack certain finesse and sometimes talent - nothing that cannot be learned!

In this case, there are tips to help you become more successful! It is not necessary to episode everything dogmatically - everyone is different. In player A tactic A works, where player B reaps failures with tactic A. Over time you will find out which tactic is best for you.

key elements

There are such "little things" like skill in shooting, physical condition or a basic understanding of the rules of the game. If one of these aspects is missing, you compensate with the others or accept worse results.

Develop skills

You don't have to train all the time! Most players have a job, a girlfriend, study or have other obligations.

In all these cases there is no time, it is impossible to read every military book and do physical training in parallel. Take smaller steps. Observe where your deficits are and focus on them!

Start getting more involved with Airsoft. Start a fitness workout that's right for you. Practice with the indoor shooting box. At the beginning, it's not absolute perfection that counts, but a sensitization for the training topic.

Stay consistently on it. Use the power of habit to your advantage! It's never too late to start!

Learn sparks

Most teams have radios in place. If you train in a team, it makes sense to think about sparking.

Handy, cheap radios are now available for very little money in stores. They offer different application possibilities, are cheap and good to trade. You need a user manual (unless you know the models), charger and/or batteries and the matching headset (if you think you can play freely). With a matching headset, you can get started. A good, cheap model is the "Midland G7". For men, throat mics are suitable for speaking - for women, it's less suitable because of its smaller throat!

Train it

Military thinking means - keep things short and compact! Today, this applies primarily to the classic funk alphabet! It helps to pass on terms or information that are difficult to understand! Useful here is a typical spelling table like the modern American version.

A	Alpha	J	Juliette	S	Sierra
B	Bravo	K	Kilo	T	Tango
C	Charlie	L	Lima	U	Uniform
D	Delta	M	Mike	V	Victor
E	Echo	N	November	W	Whisky
F	Foxtrott	O	Oscar	X	X-Ray
G	Golf	P	Papa	Y	Yankee
H	Hotel	Q	Quebec	Z	Zulu
I	India	R	Romeo		

- ➢ Speak slowly and clearly
- ➢ Spell heavy words when needed
- ➢ No naming - this helps to clarify in advance who carries which "code" - e.g. - player Timothy becomes Alpha2, player Angus becomes DeltaX,...
- ➢ Use abbreviations that only you know!
- ➢ In other words, if it is necessary or important - and the information can only be conveyed in this way.
- ➢ Keep the conversation short.
- ➢ Say short and concise - refrain from phrases or courtesy formulas like "please and thank you!
- ➢ Formulate the information briefly and clearly understandable.
- ➢ First press, then speak - otherwise, you will get cut off sentences.
- ➢ Confirm with an agreed term like "OK" or "Understood".

Train several times until the radio discipline is in place!

Handling the marker

The marker is a central component in airsoft sports. Although some countries have markers as "toys" in the law, proper use of them will help you achieve a better player episode.

If you orientate yourself on real weapons when dealing with markers, you will be a giant step ahead of many players.

What's included?

> ➢ Security guidelines
> ➢ carrying method
> ➢ Loading and unloading activities
> ➢ types of attacks
> ➢ Fault detection and elimination

The goal of this "weapon drill" is the safe control of your marker and to internalize it in the form of an "automatism".

The weapon drill teaches you the basic skills necessary for excellent firing behaviour. It is, like everything else, to practice until the movements arrive in the muscle memory. If you master the exercises almost asleep, you have a huge advantage over other players!

<u>safety guidelines</u>

One of the most important "rules" in real weapons sport is the "safety rules according to Jeff Cooper". They serve the general security and are not to be neglected in Airsoft, only because they are not real weapons, but markers.

Security rules according to Jeff Cooper

Jeff Cooper former Marine Lieutenant Colonel served in World War II and the Korean War before retiring from active military service in 1956.

In 1976, he started training military and police personnel, as well as civilians, on firearms of all kinds.

He joined the four basic rules of modern firearms security:

1. All firearms are **always** loaded.
   (Even if they are not, consider them as if they wer.)
2. Never point the muzzle at something you do not want to fire at.
   (For cases where the weapon appears to be unloaded, see rule 1)
3. Keep your finger away from the trigger until the sights are clearly aligned with the target..
   (This is the golden rule. The violation of this rule is the main cause of unwanted firing.)

4. Identify the target and background.
   (Don't shoot something you haven't identified for sure.)

In simpler terms, the rules say:

1. Consider EVERY weapon loaded.
2. Aim the muzzle only at what you really want to shoot at.
3. Touch the trigger with your fingers only when you want to shoot.
4. Be sure of your target and what is behind it.

In simpler terms, the rules say!

For experienced players, certain rules of conduct have become flesh and blood. Beginners often lack this knowledge. If you follow these simple safety rules, you are on the safe side!

- ✓ *ALWAYS wear your eye protection!*
  In the playground (and in the safe zone) it is better to wear glasses. This will protect you and your eyesight. A ricochet happens quickly.
- ✓ *Never point the muzzle at something you don't want to shoot at.*
  Watch your muzzle control! This will prevent you from accidentally hurting anyone! It also minimizes the risk of „friendly fire".
- ✓ *Unload your marker when you are outside the game.*
  Wait until you are on the playing field -> first plug in the magazine there. Leave the playing field -> take out the

magazine and shoot towards the ground so that no BB is left in the barrel! It doesn't matter if you just fetch something or "used up" your last life and are out of the game.

✓ *Don't shoot something you haven't identified.*

Don't shoot something you haven't identified.

Even if you have opted for a machine gun like the M60 or the M249 - blind shooting only makes limited sense. In the middle of the action you may have no other choice, but pure "spray and pray" is more of a BB waste!

The same goes for blind shooting over an obstacle or behind a wall! Learn to shoot precisely and well.

✓ *Don't just rely on safety systems!*

Do you know "Murphys Rules"? These say - What can go wrong, goes wrong. Airsoft markers have a range of safety systems and modules, both mechanical and electrical. Although they are designed to prevent unwanted firing, there is a possibility of safety systems malfunctioning.

Treat your marker as if it were loaded to minimize this risk.

✓ *Take precautions if your marker does not shoot.*

If a marker doesn't work or is bumpy, you rarely know the reason immediately.

A forgotten battery, non-functioning gears or a marker that is too dry will prevent you from performing well. If this problem cannot be solved immediately, remove the magazine, secure the marker and play with your backup marker.

Take a closer look at it in the safe zone (or at home).
Time and rest will help you make the right diagnosis!

✓ *Use matching BB*
Cheap BBs carry the risk of damage!

✓ *Clean the barrel of the marker*
Clean him regularly! To do this, aim the barrel against the ground on the playing field and pull the trigger. Think about a more thorough cleaning after the match day! With a cleaned barrel you increase your hit accuracy and prevent catches!

✓ *Learn how markers work.*
The knowledge about how markers work is useful to recognize if your marker causes problems or doesn't work as desired.

✓ *Gain experience if you want to rebuild your marker!*
In the Airsoft community there are absolute professionals who can perfect any marker. Beginners usually lack experience. First conversion attempts rarely work.

types of attacks

A good, cleanly executed stroke helps you in the game. You become more unerring! Here you can see three commonly used strokes.

Single-handed stroke or single-handed grip

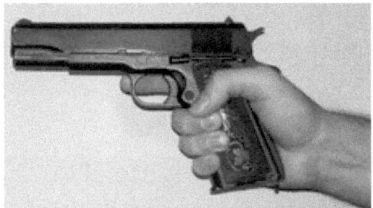 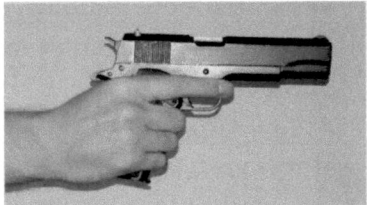

Two-handed stop or two-handed handle

 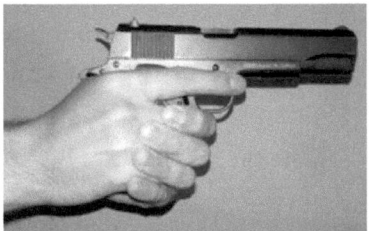

Two-handed stop - hands together

 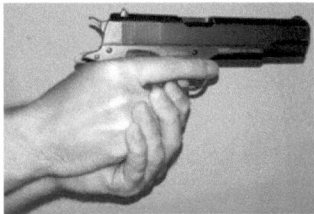

In addition, there are different positions, with whose help you can also improve your shooting skills.

Ready position

In the standby position, you can hold the marker either towards the floor or towards the ceiling/sky.

Shooting position

You hold the marker in place with both hands. Bend your knees slightly for a more stable stand.

Ducked with both hands

In this position, you duck relatively low, so it can be exhausting.

Over the left shoulder

Make sure you have a stable position and that both legs carry your balance well balanced.

Kneeling with both hands

This position is comfortable for longer periods. You can squat on the heel of one leg and support yourself on the knee of the other leg.

Lying

Make sure to extend your heels parallel to the ground!

The stop refers to the posture of the body and weapons when shooting. Everyone trains one or two personal favorites. Don't panic if you don't know them yet. Sometimes it takes some time!

Tips for handicrafts

for Indoor training

Even in the smallest apartment there is room - and if it is little. You don't even have to leave the apartment for shooting exercises, as long as you take care of the necessary materials.

You will need your marker, BBs, an indoor firing range and suitable targets.

Indoor firing range

You can find similar shooting modules in the real weapons scene. This Airsoft model is an adapted version of it. What is good for real gun shooters, is available in a modified version for Airsoft players.

You can use this indoor shooting box in your own home to train different movements, shoot in a marker or just have fun.

Required material:

- ✓ 1 moderately large wooden box
- ✓ 1 larger plate packing material (old cartons)
- ✓ 1 Tucker with ammunition
- ✓ 1 Stanley knife
- ✓ 1 old mattress or larger foam rubber pieces

First place the wooden box with the opening upwards. Take the cardboard plate, place it on the wooden box and cut the pages with the Stanley knife to size. Make sure it covers all four sides of the box.

Cut a piece from the mattress that you can easily fit into the wooden box. Make sure it sits and does not come loose by itself.

Place the cardboard plate on the open side and chug at the edges. Fix the targets on this plate later.

Tip:

Have several cardboard plates ready in a suitable size. Over time, you won't be able to avoid replacing them. The same applies to the mattress pieces.

Airsoft shooting targets

For training with your indoor shooting box, you need targets! With practice, you will achieve a better performance than most other beginners!

Training with an indoor shooting box is a great way to burn motion sequences into your muscle memory. This includes, for example, safety and ejection or hits accuracy. The better the automatic in the muscle memory works, the more you can concentrate on your opponents in the game.

> ## *Free downloadable pictures*
> Pick a target you like and print it on an A4 page. The variety is enormous, the price factor is negligible. Fix it with a Tucker or adhesive tape on the cardboard plate of your indoor shooting box.

> ## *Finished Prints*
> You can get these in gun shops or air shops.

General Tips

If you wish to be good at Airsoft, adapt Drill to military training.

It doesn't mean anymore, because of sustainable practice and repetition in handling!

Training to ensure success

If you think about military drill for your training, use these phrases to your advantage:

1. _entry phase_
   repeat exercises to secure what you have learned
2. _learning phase_
   acquire new knowledge and/or skills without time pressure and develop solutions to questions that arise
3. _application phase_
   repeat what you have learned so far and apply it as realistically as possible
4. _consolidation phase_
   Automate what you have learned by repeating it all the time

Use a handful of simple exercise rules:

- ➤ What's important to you helps you - it makes sense to you, which increases your training success. Search for subjective significance in new knowledge.

- ➤ Prefer meaningful, structured content over disjointed information.
- ➤ Combine new information with existing knowledge, so that you can better keep in mind what you have learned.
- ➤ Increase your training success by regularly repeating what you have learned.

Basically, you use a limited, temporal component to achieve a goal you want!

The more meaningful the training is for you, the better these things will be memorized in your mind. During training, many people tend to overlook this aspect. The more you embed your "learning to do" in a suitable, meaningful overall context, the easier it is for you to remember various elements.

If you take over military inspired drill for your training, you primarily repeat movement sequences in connection with markers and acquire practical as well as theoretical knowledge.

"Military" basic skills will help you get a better result on the field! This does not mean that you are mentally shutting down or idling! We are not talking about almost meditative running conditions here! This is something completely different!

Effect of the Drill

Imagine you are in the middle of the game and need a new magazine quickly. Once you have succeeded in switching to automatic mode, you will be supplied with new ammunition within a few moments. Otherwise, you are under stress, your hands tremble and you try to pull the new magazine with fresh ammunition out of your pocket and put it into the marker.

Drill-trained skills, knowledge, and behaviors look like driving a car. You'll automatically move and focus on the situation per se.

Mastering matter as if you were asleep increases confidence in yourself and your own abilities. You have additional thinking capacities and act reflexively.

Think about football training. The coaches constantly go through certain standard situations with the footballers. This is also drill, but more sporty and not military! The same applies to musicians or chess players. Even when learning Languages you will find something similar!

Practical training can be divided into four levels in the military sense:

> *Preparation and instruction*
> Are all materials available? Are they available in the correct series episode? What is "training objective"?
> *Demonstrating and explaining*

[75]

Is there a trainer who can help? Are you dependent on literature and/or Youtube videos?

➤ *How exactly does the exercise work?*
Study the movement sequences! If something is unclear to you, ask for possibilities!

➤ *Subdivide the thing into short, simple sections.*
Divide the project and/or the exercise into simple steps. Go forward step by step until you master everything.

➤ *Copying and explaining*
Try what you see. Most exercises require a certain minimum amount of time for perfect control. If someone is standing next to you to support you, ask if you are insecure. An incorrectly rehearsed exercise is difficult to correct.

➤ *Completion and independent practice*
If you are sure about the exercise, repeat it when you find the time. The more often you repeat, the faster you master the exercise! In this way, you train and consolidate your knowledge and skills!

Easier winning!

In the beginning, the fun of playing dominates. Within a short period of time, many players ask themselves about the possibilities for increased chances of winning. Although the first thought usually means improved tuning, there are far more efficient, cheaper methods!

Analyze your own playing behavior. Do you like to storm forward or hold back? Do you carry heavy equipment or are you rather lighter packed?

Keep profile small

The less visible you are, the smaller the hit area you offer your opponents. Keep your elbows close to you! In the CQB you act the same way! Get on your knees. Keep your body as far behind covers as possible.

Attention!
If you are in a ditch or ducked, other players usually discover your head first. What alternatives to head hits do you offer them?

Use Coverages

Keep yourself and your body covered. Use the possibilities you have - bunkers, huts, barn, bales of straw or fallen trees don't matter. Use any cover you can get.

Keep in mind that with many types of cover, the view outside is hardly possible. Here it depends on the type of cover you have. Just because you don't see your opponent doesn't mean he doesn't notice you in your hiding place. Keep your eyes and ears open. If an opponent believes himself unobserved, he acts more carelessly.

Covers are suitable for bunkering and defending. At the same time, they develop into traps under certain circumstances. Learn to assess which covers are practical and which are less suitable for you and your playing style.

Look around corners

How you do it is up to you. Use smaller mirrors, a CD, a periscope or keep your head out of sight for a moment.

If a swing BB comes towards you, you know at least one opponent is nearby and ready to kick you out of the game.

Minimize your weight

It depends on you and your playing style.

Players tend to pick up all sorts of equipment and materials. Soon the awakening comes - it's too hard to make it all day.

Learn to slim down. Drop unnecessary equipment, gear and miscellaneous. Think about what you need and what dead ballast is.

Learn to shoot more professionally

Use videos or textbooks, ask someone to teach you "more professional shooting" or practice with an indoor shooting box.

Shooting with real weapons makes little sense in order to achieve better shooting results in Airsoft. Rebound and distance are too different compared to Airsoft and real weapons. However, the handling of a real weapon is transferable to a marker.

Learn how to add tunings yourself

Many players are technical anti-geniuses. Others touch a marker and know what it has. How good are you at technical things?

If you have a certain basic understanding of technology, you'll want to look at the inner workings of your marker. Tuned markers sometimes reach the limit of perfection. They are more accurate and achieve greatly improved performance and hit rate.

Most beginners faced similar questions to you. Talent, skill, and ability, as well as the depth of your wallet and personal interests, helped some Airsoft players to absolute expert status in tuning.

The more you can tune and repair yourself, the more independent you are of others!

"Running Cadence"

Bars help you walk. The military has long recognized this.

You often see a troop running in movies, one screams a text and the others yell after the same words.

It doesn't matter if you choose a piece of music and listen to it, or if you run together and one of you pretends the lyrics!

Pay attention to the constant beat and try it out!

Feel how the rhythm penetrates you, how you begin to put your feet on the ground in a certain beat.

Your heart and feet begin to move in unison.

When you reach this state, you run better, further and faster. Why do so many runners wear earplugs and listen to music? They have recognized this little trick.

Marine Corps Marching Cadence

Back in 1775

Back in 1775
My Marine Corps came alive
First there came the color gold
To show the world that we are bold
Then there came the color red
To show the world the blood we shed
Then there came the color green
To show the world that we are mean
Then there came the color blue
To show the world that we are true
Oh yeah
Marine Corps
Your corps
My corps

Army Running Cadence

Momma Momma Cant you see?

mama mama can't you see,
what the army's done to me.

They put me in a barber's chair,
spun me around I had no hair.

Mama mama can't you see,
what the army's done to me.

They took away my favorite jeans,
now I'm wearing army greens.

Mama mama can't you see,
what the army's done to me.

I use to date beauty queens,
now I love my M16.

Mama mama can't you see,
what the army's done to me.

I use to drive a Cadalliac,
now I carry one on my back.

Air Force Marching Cadence

What the Air Force has Done to Me

Chorus:
Whoa, whoa, whoa, whoa
Whoa, whoa, I gotta go
Whoa, whoa, whoa, whoa
Whoa, whoa, I gotta go
Momma, momma, can't you see
what the Air Force's done to me
Momma,momma, can't you see
what the Air Force's done to me
Chorus
They took away my faded jeans
Now I'm wearing Air Force greens
Used to drive a Cadillac
Now I hump it on my back
Used to date a beauty queen
Now I hug my M-16
Used to drive a Chevrolet
Now I'm walking all the way

Navy Running Cadence

Whacha ya wanna be – Pilot

When I was in first grade my teacher said to me
Whacha gonna do boy, whacha gonna be
A policeman, a fireman, a football star
You got a lot a' tallent boy, your gonna go far
I wanna be a pilot
Gonna be a pilot
Flyin' for the Navy
That's what I'm gonna be.

When I was in high school my teacher said to me
Whacha gonna do boy, whacha gonna be
A doctor, a lawyer, an engineer
You know you're gonna go really far from here
I wanna be a pilot
Gonna be a pilot
Flyin' for the Navy
That's what I'm gonna be.

Watch your breath!

Breathing influences your shooting results! This point applies to you especially if you want to play a sniper!

Have you already fired with real weapons? Experienced real weapon shooters know it's wiser to control their breath if you want good results.

Chest or abdominal breathing?

Do you pay attention to your breath? Most people do this when they are cold and their glasses mist up. Sagittarians often learn to control their breath. In everyday life, people breathe in both versions. If you act as a sniper, breathing control can help you additionally.

> *Breast Breathing*
  Activates the bodily functions
> *abdominal breathing*
  Dampens the excitement

In Airsoft your body needs more oxygen due to increased movement and exertion. The absorption capacity is linked to your endurance training condition! Endurance training increases your receptivity and pushes the limits of your performance backward. The lower your endurance level, the more likely your body is to need additional oxygen!

Breathing technique

Learn to control your breath! The best way is to take your shot between two breaths. The better you can control your breath, the better your shot results will develop!

- ✓ Use abdominal breathing primarily.
- ✓ Take a deep breath and ensure a good oxygen supply in the blood!
- ✓ Aim carefully and squeeze between two heartbeats.

You will be calmer, your hands will tremble less and the probability of a hit will increase.

If you concentrate on abdominal breathing before you pull the trigger, a better hit rate is more likely! Learn to breathe correctly early on. In the heat of the game, very few players pay attention!

Observe yourself in the game:

- ✓ How do you breathe?
- ✓ Do you use abdominal or thoracic breathing?
- ✓ How do your muscles feel? Are they tense or tense?

Initially breathe normally. As a rule, you use chest breathing. This supplies the body with a certain amount of oxygen and thus prevents an undersupply!

Switch slowly from chest to abdominal breathing. Breathing becomes flatter. Start now with goals! After firing the shot, breathe in and out deeply several times. The body again has the normal amount of oxygen for you.

Simple tricks

- ✓ Breathe consciously through your stomach!
- ✓ Relax!
- ✓ Pay attention to a relaxed posture
- ✓ Put your hand on your belly and feel your belly move.

When breathing, think "On", "Off", "Rest".

Have fun on training!

Learn to aim!

Do you keep both eyes or one eye open when you sight? Trained shooters (especially snipers) use both eyes for aiming and shooting.

If both eyes are open, the brain has to process two different images and combine them to a whole. The more dominant eye produces a stronger image.

Do you know your dominant eye?

Fix a point! Make a triangle with your hands! Keep looking through this triangle at the point. Close one eye first and open it again. Close the other eye and open it again.

At which eye did you stay closer to the fixed point? This is your dominant eye!

Try out how comfortable it is for you to keep one eye closed for a longer period of time. You use muscles to pinch the eye. To focus, this effort is added. This makes your eyes tired more quickly. If you open the eye again, the problem of different brightness levels is added. An eye must adapt. If you leave both eyes open, it will take getting used to, but it will be less tiring in the long run.

Standing correctly

Are you right when you're holding a marker in your hands?

Have you thought about how standing correctly affects your hit rate? Touch technique and "real standing" play together. Take a look at the photos on pages 64 - 66. Look at the leg and arm positions. Every position has its reason!

There are situations in which you can calmly lay down on your opponent. If you are in a hiding place and can dock in peace and quiet, peace and quiet, the right touch and suitable standing pays off!!

Procedure

Spread your weight evenly on both legs. Make sure your feet are shoulder-wide, press your knees a little and keep your hips straight. Bend your upper body slightly back, relax your shoulders. Hold your head upright and bend it towards the marker.

Place your upper arm slightly against your upper body and keep your wrists straight. Raise your elbow slightly. Leave your shoulders loose.

This will give you a well-balanced balance.   Take several deep breaths. Relax! Find the pressure point! Exhale gently! Now you are ready to take the perfect shot!

[89]

The perfect shot

You've now learned a few things that will help you improve your Airsoft performance. Many players dream of the "perfect hit", but few of them manage it regularly. If you never train, you can't expect superior performance - no matter how much you spend on your equipment.

It's already a matter of time to practice in real weapon sports until the perfect shot is fired. Airsoft players sometimes have a harder time. For example, they have to take lighter ammunition and different movement sequences into account.

The best shooting technique is the one you hit best!

Just like in real gun sport, the perfect shot counts in Airsoft!

- ✓ Learn to use your target equipment sensibly. A sinfully expensive rifle scope will not help you if you cannot handle it.
- ✓ Practice shooting regularly! For example, use an indoor shooting range at home!
- ✓ Internal movement sequences and automates them!
- ✓ Use sensible breathing techniques!
- ✓ Pay attention to the correct posture!
- ✓ Criteria: Stability, naturalness and practiced execution
- ✓ Pay attention to grip, stop and trigger behavior.
- ✓ Aim without trembling and pull the trigger at the right moment.

✓ Train yourself the right trigger control. Adjust the moment between heartbeats before firing.

A very good player learns techniques to land a perfect shot.

A miserable player, on the other hand, will not be helped by the most expensive equipment!

epilog

Many clubs offer group training, concentrating on a handful of components. Good training includes several aspects - physical, mental and team training.

Be patient with yourself. Training episode takes time! Allow yourself and your body the necessary time. Don't expect miracles, success will come over time if you "stay tuned".

Don't expect too much at once. Man is a creature of habit. If you are more of a "Couch Potatoe" type at the moment, you won't be acting like a "Special Forces Member" within a week.

Most special forces need weeks to bring their people to a high level - and they don't have to work 40 hours and run a household parallel to training!

Find your personal pace and rhythm! Just because some say this or that time is the best doesn't mean it's the best time for you! Find your own optimal training conditions!

Check your progress regularly

✓ *What do you want to achieve by when?*
Which ultimate goal do you have in mind? Break this goal down to smaller steps. This will make it easier for you to stay on the ball!

✓ *Do I make mistakes?*
Mistakes can happen to anyone. There is nothing wrong with that. You learn from it! Pay attention to what you do wrong and correct it!

✓ *What do you want to improve?*
Doesn't your training run according to your wishes? What can you change to make it your way?

✓ *How do others proceed?*
Watch videos, talk to other players and learn! Take what you like and work on perfecting this aspect.

✓ *Have you already internalized the steps?*
About every step until it sits. Each movement requires a number of repetitions until it feels completely natural to you.

✓ *Have you practiced everything correctly?*
Check what you have learned. Record yourself on video or ask someone to watch you. Are the movements right?

✓ *Are there improvements?*
If so, then praise yourself. Grant yourself a reward! Afterward, you go to the next step!